Steps To Success

(A Key to Success Creativity)

By

Blessed Thabang Mobosi

i

Steps to Success

Steps to Success

Published by
William Jenkins
2503 - 4288 Grange Street
Burnaby BC V5H 1P2
Canada

williamhenryjenkins@gmail.com
http://williamjenkins.ca
Cell: 1-778-928-6139

ISBN 13: 978-1-928164-21-0
ISBN 10: 1928164218

Steps to Success

Dedication

I dedicate this book to my creator the almighty God. Thanks for the Solomonic wisdom and knowledge from above.

Steps to Success

Steps to Success

Author
Blessed Thabang Mobosi

Blessed Thabang Mobosi was born in 1997 on December 17th. He lives in South Africa with his parents, two young brothers and one sister.

He believes that his calling is to become a Financial Manager. He hopes to study Commerce and Finance in university and specialize in Financial Management as a career. As well, he wants to be an International Evangelist. His role model is Dag Heward Mills. He completed his Bible basic school in 2012 and his prayer school on 2013 and graduated as a disciple in 2014. He was ordained as a minister In Jubilee Christian Church where he served as a youth leader for 13 years. He also served as the Chairperson of the Student Christian Organization of Ritavi Circuit in Mopani District, Limpopo, South Africa for 3 years when 26 schools were under his leadership. As well, he served at Hudson Ntsanwisi Senior Secondary School for 5 years as Chairperson of their Student Christian Organization.

He is a preacher and motivator, a mentor of a number of youth including young adults. He is a singer and a keyboardist and an inspiration to his community. When he was eleven, he started to preach and motivate students at primary level at Ritavi Primary School located at in Nkowankowa, Limpopo, South Africa.

He wishes to reach out to the world with his motivational sermons, poems and speeches. He has been invited on many different occasions to act as minister. You can catch him at:

Email: Blessed.btm@gmail.com

Contact: +27 61 953 9726 or
+27 78 506 5555

Facebook Page: Author Blessed Thabang Mobosi
Web site: http://amazon.com/author/blessedmobosi

Acknowledgements

My thanks to my mentor Mrs. Maholovela for your improvements to my life; and to my wonderful teachers at Hudson Ntsanwisi Senior Secondary School who have always inspired me and motivated me always to go the extra mile; and to friends and mentees.

My thanks to Mr. William Jenkins, my publisher from Canada. Thanks for the great acceptance of my first book "Destiny is a Matter of Choice" and my Second Book, "The Power Of Determination". Long life unto you, Sir.

To my wonderful parents Mr Antony Mobosi & Rosina Mothopane Mobosi, my father and mother. Thanks for your support. Your harvest in my success awaits you.

Steps To Success

Steps To Success

Table of Contents

Dedication v

Author vii

Acknowledgements..ix

Introduction 1

    Attitude Change 2

        Positive Attitude.. 2

        Negative Attitude 3

    Why Your Attitude Is So Important................................ 4

    Attitude Can Be Changed 5

    Your Attitude Determines Your Success 9

    Your Attitude Largely Determines Your Expectations For The Future
.... 10

Steps for Developing a Positive Attitude 13

    Choose to be happy. 13

    Have faith in yourself 13

    Visualize 13

    Self-Coaching 13

    Self-Motivation Through Discovering Your Motives...... 14

    Always be positive.. 14

    The Power of Words 14

    Enthusiasm.. 15

    Connecting to Your Spiritual Empowerment 15

    Lighten Up Your Life with Humor................................. 15

Keep Yourself Focused 16

Steps To Success

How you can improve your ability to focus 17

Don't say you cannot focus 18

Make deals with your mind 18

Do one thing at a time 18

Things That Prevent Our Focusing 19

Be Disciplined 22

Value of Discipline... 24

Meaning Of Self-Discipline 26

Evils Of Indiscipline 27

Causes Of Indiscipline 27

Be Committed 29

Commitment Begins Small And Can Get Bigger.............. 34

Avoid your Enemy Of Success: Laziness 36

Simple Steps For Overcoming Laziness 36

Break Down A Task Into Smaller Tasks 36

Rest, Sleep And Exercise 36

Strengthen Your Willpower & Self-discipline............... 36

Motivation... 37

Have A Vision Of What And Who You Want To Be 37

Think About Benefits... 37

Thinking About The Consequences......................... 37

Doing One Thing At A Time 38

Visualization 38

Repeat Affirmations... 38

Steps To Success

Regard A Task As An Exercise.. 38

Procrastination.. 38

Learn From Successful People 39

Steps To Time Management Success.. 40

Prioritize—Put Your "Rocks" In First 40

Target Your Action 40

Focus Your Mind First 41

Take Something Off Your Plate 41

Complete Something You've Been Putting Off........................... 42

Declare Yourself Complete 42

Accept That You Can't Do It All At Once 42

Ten Steps To Your Success 44

Imagination Often Turns Into Reality...................................... 44

What You Do Every Day Will Turn Into A Habit 44

Don't Let Moods Control your Life 44

Break The Obstacles In Your Way 45

Never Lose Hope 45

Read Between The Lines 45

Take Positive Action.. 45

It Doesn't Matter Where You Live 45

Treat Your Time Like Money In The Bank 46

Adopt An Attitude Of Calmness And Of Open-Mindedness 46

No Sacrifices No Success... 47

The Ten Commandments Of Success.. 48

Steps To Success

Welcome Criticism 48

Learn From Your Failures 49

Dream Big.. 49

Always Open Your Mind To Possibilities 49

Always Be Time Conscious 49

Associate With Winners... 50

Encourage Others 50

Avoid Distractions 50

Develop The Action Habit 50

Be Patient.. 50

Follow Your Passions and Success Will Follow.................... 52

What I Mean By Passion 53

Why Passion Is So Important 53

The Successful Of Our Time 54

Steve Jobs.. 54

Chris Gardner 54

Mark Zuckerberg.. 54

Warren Buffett 55

It's Never Too Late 56

Why Success Always Starts With Failure........................... 57

The Wrong Way To React To Failure.................................. 57

Denial 57

Chasing your losses 57

Hedonism 57

Steps To Success

The Recipes For Success... 58

    Adaptation 58

    Try new things.. 58

    Recognize Failure 58

    Gather feedback... 59

    Remove emotions from the equation..................................... 59

    Don't get too attached to your plan 59

Achieving True Success And Prosperity 60

    True Success.. 60

    How Can You Develop Will For Success? 61

    Dealing Constructively With Failure...................................... 62

    Don't Do Half-Heartedly 63

    Be Creative 63

    Creating All-Round Success.. 64

    Abundance And Prosperity 65

    Affirmations For Success 66

Other Books by this Author... 68

    To order any of the books... 68

    The Publisher 68

Steps To Success

Introduction

Success is the achievement of things planned for or hoped for. They can be goals, dreams or an achievement of some kind. We all want to be successful in life, in achieving the kind of future that is our destiny. However, the truth is that not everyone will end up being successful in life. Rules can be broken, and laws can be obeyed, but success has principles of its own. Only those who cling to its principles will be successful at the end.

The fact that many are making it in the present does not mean that they will end up being successful in life, but those who are determined to the end while holding to the principles of success can be. It is not about how you start. It is not about where you are. It's about how you will be at the end of the race when you begin to face the reality of your accomplishments. Many people wish they could be successful, but they never are. Many people desire success, but they never achieve it. Whatever they wished for or desired faded away like the mist simply because they were not determined about their actions.

In this book we shall discuss the different steps to success, what makes people successful and what makes people unsuccessful. There are many ways to be successful in life, but for now, let's look unto the following:

Steps To Success

Attitude Change

Attitude is the way you feel and think about somebody or something. It decides the way you behave towards something that shows how you feel about it.

Positive Attitude

A positive attitude leads to success and happiness. A positive attitude helps you cope more easily with the daily affairs of life. It brings optimism into your life and makes it easier to avoid worries and negative thoughts. If you adopt a positive attitude as a way of life, it will bring constructive changes into your life and make your days happier, brighter and more successful. With a positive attitude, you see the bright side of life, you become optimistic, and expect the best to happen. Positive attitude manifests in the following ways:

- Positive thinking
- Constructive thinking
- Creative thinking
- Optimism
- Motivation and energy to accomplish goals
- An attitude of happiness

A positive frame of mind can help you in many ways, such as:

- Expecting success and not failure. This makes you feel inspired. It gives you the strength not to give up when you encounter obstacles on your way. It makes you look at failure and problems as blessings in disguise.
- Believing in yourself and in your abilities. This enables you to have self-esteem and confidence.

Steps To Success

- Look for solutions instead of problems.
- Recognize opportunities.

A positive attitude leads to happiness and success and can change your whole life. If you look at the bright side of life, your whole life becomes filled with light. This light affects not only you and the way you look at the world, but it also affects your environment and the people around you. If this attitude is strong enough, it becomes contagious. It is as if you radiate light around you.

Learn how to turn your dreams into reality with simple creative visualization techniques. You can improve your life, find love, attract money, and create success and much more.

Your positive attitude helps you achieve goals and attain success. It produces more energy.

Your positive attitude increases your faith in your abilities and brings hope for a brighter future. You become able to inspire and motivate yourself and others. You encounter fewer obstacles and difficulties in your daily life. You get more respect and love from people. Life smiles at you.

Negative Attitude

Negative attitude says: you cannot achieve success. Positive attitude says: You can achieve success. If you have been exhibiting a negative attitude and expecting failure and difficulties, it is now the time to change the way you think. It is the time to get rid of negative thoughts and behavior, and start leading a happier and more successful life. If you tried to do so in the past and failed, it only means that you have not tried enough.

Why Your Attitude Is So Important

The important steps you can take toward achieving your greatest potential in life are to learn to monitor your attitude and its impact on your work performance, relationships and everyone around you. In truth, people generally don't have a high level of attitude awareness. They will know if they are hungry or if their feet hurt, but they usually don't have a good handle on their attitude. That is a mistake because attitude is important. It governs the way you perceive the world and the way the world perceives you.

We all have a choice. We can choose an inner dialogue of self-encouragement and self-motivation, or we can choose one of self-defeat and self-pity. It's a power we all have. Each of us encounters hard times, hurt feelings, heartache, and physical and emotional pain. The key is to realize it's not what happens to you that matters; it's how you choose to respond.

Your mind is like a computer that can be programmed. You can choose whether the "software" installed is productive or unproductive. Your inner dialogue is the software that programs your attitude, which determines how you present yourself to the world around you. You have control over the programming. Whatever you put into it is reflected in what comes out.

Many of us have behavior patterns today that were programmed into our brains at a very tender age. The information that was recorded by our brains could have been completely inaccurate or cruel. The sad reality of life is that we will continue to hear negative information, but we don't have to program it into our brains. The loudest and most influential voice you hear is your own inner voice, your self-critic.

It can work for you or against you, depending on the messages you allow. It can be optimistic or pessimistic. It can wear you down or cheer you on. You control the sender and the receiver, but only if you consciously take responsibility for and control over your inner conversation.

Habitual bad attitudes are often the product of experiences and events. Common causes include low self-esteem, stress, fear, resentment, anger and an inability to handle change. It takes serious work to examine the roots of a harmful attitude, but the rewards of ridding ourselves of this heavy baggage can last a lifetime.

Attitude Can Be Changed

"You cannot control what happens to you, but you can control your attitude toward what happens to you, and in that, you will be mastering change rather than allowing it to master you". - Brian Tracy.

When we observe our surroundings, the environment and the people living within and around us, we learn that the world is a difficult place to live. It is not an easy task for anyone on this earth to survive and live a peaceful life. Wherever we look, we see people struggling and fighting each moment in order to achieve their goals and to be successful.

Every human being has a unique set of problems and difficulties which they are trying to overcome in order to obtain what they are striving to obtain. This constant struggle and all the obstacles that occur at every step we take become a huge cause of depression and people tend to lose heart. Then the only way to go ahead is to keep on persevering with the tasks, so that progress is made. Finally you can achieve what you have set as your goal and not leave anything half-finished.

The power and force that drives us is our attitude. A positive attitude is something that makes or breaks a person. If you have a positive outlook on life, you will always look at the positive side of things. Looking for the positives in everything you do and see will ensure that you are content and happy and live a life full of optimism and hope.

Hope is, of course, what we all live by, as no one knows what God has kept in store for us. Therefore, there is absolutely no use being negative and spreading the negativity around. By doing this we will not only damage ourselves but also damage our surroundings and the people we are related to in some way or the other.

Problems exist. They will remain there and will never go away. When we solve one problem, another one will arise, then another and another. This cycle will continue throughout our lives until we leave the earth.

Therefore, it is important that we face this life and the difficulties that arise with a positive attitude and with good will and enthusiasm. It is all about how we view the world. When things are not going well and everything seems in disarray, it is only our positive attitude that keeps us going and ensures us that it is just a phase that will pass. Thomas Jefferson says: "Nothing can stop the man with the right mental attitude from achieving his goal; nothing on earth can help the man with the wrong mental attitude".

It is actually all about our mindset. If we decide that everything is good and look for the positives, we will find that things are actually great. Similarly, if we want to see all negative, then we would find negatives and discrepancies in even the positive things in life. Hence, it is important to keep a positive mindset and outlook on life.

Kahlil Gibran says: "Your living is determined not so much by what life brings to you as by the attitude you bring to life; not so much by what happens to you as by the way your mind looks at what happens".

What needs to be done has to be done. We can either choose to do it with an unthankful and ungrateful attitude or we can do it with a smile on our face, but we have to do it in either case. Therefore, the obviously right way to go about it is to do it in a positive light and with the hope that this hard time will pass and everything will be sorted out eventually. We just need to be patient, wait for the right time and believe in our God.

There is a famous saying: "Seeing someone happy does not mean that everything in his or her life is perfect. Rather he or she has chosen to overlook the imperfections in their life". That is exactly the way how one should go about life. Humans are imperfect and therefore the world is imperfect and this is something we should learn early in our lives.

Steps To Success

If we do not accept this fact and keep getting depressed and angry about what people or external factors do to us, it will all eventually lead to total depression and total disaster. We cannot control others and we cannot change others. The only thing that we can control and change is our own attitude. Once we alter our own attitude, the world all of a sudden becomes a rosy place and everything seems to fall into place. As human beings, we need to learn to be thankful and happy in all situations. No matter what the circumstances, we should always give it our best shot and should try to see things in a positive light. Positivity literally takes all the unhappiness, pain and negativity away from our life. We always have a choice.

There is nothing that happens to us without our will and desire. If we feel good, it is because we choose to feel good and if we feel badly, it is because that's the way we want to feel. Similarly, attitude is a choice that we need to make.

We can choose to alter our attitude towards positivity or negativity and all that happens to us is because of us only. We cannot blame anyone else for the way we feel and the way we see the world. All that really matters is the fact that we give it our best shot and should not have any regrets.

So please, keep a positive attitude on life, work hard towards your goals and keep the positive attitude going under all circumstances. Eventually, we will all reach our destination and achieve our desired goals and the world will be a much better place. In the end, there is one absolutely brilliant saying that sums up everything:

Steps To Success

""Discouragement is dissatisfaction with the past, distaste for the present, and distrust of the future. It is ingratitude for the blessings of yesterday, indifference to the opportunities of today, and insecurity regarding strength for tomorrow. It is unawareness of the presence of beauty, unconcern for the needs of our fellow man, and unbelief in the promises of old. It is impatience with time, immaturity of thought, and impoliteness to God." - William A. Ward.

Your Attitude Determines Your Success

You need three things to be able to be successful: personal resources, a plan, and commitment. Of these three, commitment is the most important. If you have commitment, you will find the personal resources and you will persist until you succeed. We all have the potential within us to achieve great things with our lives.

We can be anything we want to be. I think most people would accept the findings of brain researchers that we only use a small fraction of the potential power of our minds. Most people would accept that if we are prepared to set goals, make plans, and work hard, we are likely to achieve much more with our lives. We would have the ability to build better lives for our families, and ourselves than we would if we just do the minimum required to get by.

We may know and accept these things, but that doesn't mean that we are prepared to act on this information and actually do something about it. Why is that? I think that the alternatives are often just too attractive and easy to pursue than to put in the work necessary to achieve our goals. It may not be that difficult to put in the extra effort required that could make a big difference in our lives, but the reality is that it's much easier not go the easier softer way. There is one overriding factor that makes the difference and determines our actions, and that is our attitude. Our attitude is the deciding factor to what we experience in life and the attainment of our goals in so many areas of our life. If your attitude toward your job is that you aren't prepared to do anything outside your job description, or even less if possible, you may feel pleased by getting one over on the boss, but you're unlikely to be considered for a promotion.

Many people enter into a personal relationship with the attitude that because they've been hurt in the past, they are likely to be hurt again. It's this attitude more than anything else that will insure that these predictions are likely to come true. If you approach problems with a "why does this always happen to me" attitude (a victim mentality), you're likely to not only attract problems, but also have difficulty dealing with them.

Your Attitude Largely Determines Your Expectations For The Future

Your attitude towards what you want from your life, and what you are prepared to do to ensure you achieve your goals in life matter. If your attitude is 'what's the point?' or 'it's not worth the effort' you're sure to be proven right. By the opposite also holds true. If you're prepared to make more of an effort in your job, it's likely that this will be noticed and you will attract promotion and growth opportunities. If your attitude is generally optimistic and you don't expect to experience problems, you're not only less likely to do so, but when you do, you'll most likely find solutions more easily so you can quickly get back on track. If you have a positive attitude and look forward to every day for the opportunities it will bring, you will find more opportunities.

If you write down your goals, you will make the plans necessary to achieve your goals and take appropriate action. You are well on your way to achieving your ideal life. With an attitude of positive expectation, you will not only achieve more, but you will also experience more satisfaction in your daily life.

Others can influence our attitudes, e.g. the media, our choice of friends, and our relatives. We are also affected by our life experiences. Unfortunately, it often seems there are more negative than positive influences. We cannot control other people or events, and things will happen that we don't like that may affect us in some way, but what we can and must control is how we react to these things.

No person or event can control or change our attitude unless we allow it to do so. Likewise, no one else can really cause us to become upset or angry. When this happens, we are giving other people control over our lives and relinquishing control of our most basic human right: the control of our own mind. I'm sure you've all seen those signs in offices that go something like 'Everyone brings joy to this office, some when they enter, and some when they leave.' Which one of these people would you like to be known as? Would you like to be known as a person whose attitude gives the impression they are walking around with a permanent rain cloud over their head or would you rather be known as someone people look forward to seeing? Which person has a happier and more fulfilling life?

Steps To Success

A wise man once said, something like 'it's not your aptitude, but your attitude, that determines your altitude.' If your attitude is not working for you, it's probably working against you. Your attitude can be holding you back in ways you don't even realize. No one else can control your attitude; it's all up to you. Change your attitude and change your life.

Steps for Developing a Positive Attitude

Choose to be happy.

Yes, it is a matter of choice. When negative thoughts enter your mind, just refuse to look at them, doing your best to substitute them with happy thoughts Look at the bright side of life. It's a matter of choice and repeated attempts. Choose to be optimistic. Find reasons to smile more often. You can find such reasons, if you search for them and associate yourself with happy people

Have faith in yourself

Have faith in yourself and believe that the universe can help you.

Visualize

Visualize only what you want to happen, not what you don't want. The Power of Visualization Studies of the psychology of peak performance have found that most great athletes, surgeons, engineers and artists use affirmations and visualizations either consciously or subconsciously to enhance and focus their skills. Nelson Mandela has written extensively on how visualization helped him maintain a positive attitude while being imprisoned for 27 years. "I thought continually of the day when I would walk free. I fantasized about what I would like to do," he wrote in his autobiography. Visualization works well to improve attitude.

Self-Coaching

Affirmations repeated several times each day, every day, serve to reprogram your subconscious with positive thinking. An affirmation is made up of words charged with power, conviction and faith. You send a positive response to your subconscious, which accepts whatever you tell it. When done properly, this triggers positive feelings that, in turn, drive action.

Self-Motivation Through Discovering Your Motives

Discover what motivates you—what incites you to take action to change your life. Basic motives include love, self-preservation, anger, financial gain and fear. Self-motivation requires enthusiasm, a positive outlook, a positive physiology (walk faster, smile, sit up), and a belief in yourself and your God-given potential.

Always be positive

Attitude talk is a way to override your past negative programming by erasing or replacing it with a conscious, positive internal voice that helps you face new directions. Your internal conversation—that little voice you listen to all day long—acts like a seed in that it programs your brain and affects your behavior. Take a closer look at what you are saying to yourself.

The Power of Words

WOW once released to the universe, our words cannot be taken back. Learn the concept of WOW—watch our words. What we speak reflects what is already in our hearts based upon all the things we have come to believe about ourselves. If we find ourselves speaking judgmental and disparaging things about our circumstances or those around us, we know the condition of our hearts needs to change. You can create a direct path to success by what you say. When people ask me how I am doing, I say, "Super-fantastic." Most people enjoy working and living with others who try to live life for what it is—a beautiful gift.

Steps To Success

Enthusiasm

A vital tool for staying motivated, enthusiasm is to attitude what breathing is to life. Enthusiasm enables you to apply your gifts more effectively. It's the burning desire that communicates commitment, determination and spirit. Enthusiasm means putting yourself in motion. It's an internal spirit that speaks through your actions from your commitment and your belief in what you are doing. It is one of the most empowering and attractive characteristics you can have.

Connecting to Your Spiritual Empowerment

The ultimate level of human need extends into the spiritual realm. Just as we feed our bodies in response to our primary need to survive physically, we need to feed our spirit because we are spiritual beings. Many people find powerful and positive motivation in their faith. I happen to be one of them.

Lighten Up Your Life with Humor

Humor is a powerful motivator. The more humor and laughter in your life, the less stress you'll have, which means more positive energy to help you put your attitude into action. There are also health benefits to lightening up.

Keep Yourself Focused

To focus means to give attention or effort on one particular object, situation or person rather than another. The root cause of many failures in life is lack of focus. Attention is like a searchlight; when its beam is spread over a vast area, its power to focus on a particular object becomes weak, but focused on one thing at a time, it becomes powerful.

Great men are men of focus. They put their whole mind on one thing at a time. Man should know the scientific method of focus by which he may disengage his attention from objects of distraction and turn it upon one thing at a time. By the power of focus, man can use the untold power of mind to accomplish that which he desires and he can guard all doors through which failure may enter. We should approach our nearest problem or duty with focused energy and execute it to perfection. This should be our philosophy of life.

Focusing is the key to success. It implies, first, an ability to release one's thoughts and emotions from all other interests and involvements, and second, an ability to direct them towards a single object or state of awareness. Focusing may assume various manifestations, from a dynamic outpouring of energy to perfectly quiescent perceptions. On every level of mental activity, it is not generally known is that a concentrated mind succeeds not only because it can solve problems with greater dispatch, but also because problems have a way of somehow vanishing before its focused energies, without even requiring to be solved.

Steps To Success

A focused mind often attracts opportunities for success that, to less focused individuals, appear to come by sheer luck. A person whose mind is focused receives inspirations in his work and in his thinking. Focusing awakens our powers and channels them, dissolving obstacles in our path, attracting opportunities, insights, and inspirations. In many ways, focus is the single most important key to success.

Focus and pay attention? Paying attention to what you are doing is one of the most important keys to success. If you are not able to hold your attention on one thing for some time, how can you accomplish anything? Successful people are able to focus their mind on their goals day and night until they accomplish them, be it money, fame, power, self-improvement or meditation.

How you can improve your ability to focus

How can you improve your ability to focus your mind on your goals, when there are so many things that distract your attention? Napoleon Hill said the following words about attention: "Controlled attention is the act of coordinating all the faculties of the mind and directing their combined power to a given end. It is an act, which can be achieved only by the strictest sort of self-discipline."

"Learn to fix your attention on a given subject for whatever length of time you choose. You will have learned the secret to power and plenty! This is Focus."

"Keep your mind on the things you want and off the things you don't want!"

Steps To Success

This is good advice for any person who wishes to learn how to improve their focusing and attention. Here are several steps you can take on this important subject.

Don't say you cannot focus

Telling yourself that you cannot concentrate only makes it more difficult. By doing so, you program your mind to lack of concentration and attention. Whenever you need to focus your mind, tell yourself over and over again that you can concentrate. Tell yourself that you can develop this ability. Remember that in order to improve your focus you need to train it, as with any other skill. If you persevere and are earnest, in time you will be able to focus your mind on anything you want.

Make deals with your mind

If there is something that is distracting your attention, such as an emotional problem or an unresolved business problem, tell your mind that all these problems can wait for a little while and that you will attend to them after you finish what you are doing. If this does not help you, then write down on a piece of paper what problems you have to think about or solve. This will, to some extent, temporarily remove the problems from your mind.

Do one thing at a time

Jumping from one thing to another will only teach your mind to be inattentive and lose attention quickly. Besides that, this kind of mental restlessness can be tiring in the end. When you focus your attention on anything, be alert, and when you find yourself thinking on something else, try to stay patient and bring your mind to the subject repeatedly. Often, when you remember, try to fix your attention on whatever you happen to be doing at the moment.

Michael Leboeuf said: "When you write down your ideas you automatically focus your full attention on them. Few if any of us can write one thought and think another at the same time. Thus a pencil and paper make excellent concentration tools." "I think the one lesson I have learned is that there is no substitute for paying attention."

Diane Sawyer said: "Where attention goes, energy flows and results show."

T. Harv Eker said: "Excellence is in the details. Give attention to the details and excellence will come."

Does your attention often wander away? Are you unable to focus your mind? Learn how to improve your focus and strengthen your focusing skills.

Things That Prevent Our Focusing

Do you find it difficult to hold your attention fixed on one subject or thought longer than a few seconds before getting distracted by other thoughts or sense impressions? There are several obstacles to focusing that everyone faces, but these obstacles can be surmounted.

These are the obstacles to focusing:

- Lack of enough willpower

- Lack of enough self-discipline

- Impatient undisciplined mind

- Too much interest in other thoughts

Steps To Success

- Physical and mental restlessness

- Lack of understanding of what focusing is

- Lack of motivation to improve the focusing

- Too much stress and lack of enough rest

There are other obstacles to focusing, but these are the main ones. In order to overcome these obstacles to focus, you need to develop and strengthen your willpower and self-discipline through appropriate exercises. You can find a few exercises in my book "The Power Of Determination". If you wish to gain real inner strength, get that book and study and practice the exercises.

Through those exercises, you will discipline your mind and thoughts and overcome impatience and restlessness. Thinking often about the benefits of gaining the ability to focus and focus your mind can help too, as well as repeating affirmations about your desire to improve this ability. This will strengthen your motivation and desire, and help you overcome the obstacles on the way.

Practicing some physical exercises during the day will improve your health and your ability to overcome physical restlessness. It is also important to learn to give yourself some rest during the day, and give yourself enough sleep at night. Try to stay calm and relaxed during the day, no matter what happens. Exhibiting some inner detachment would help. Don't let yourself be too affected by what people say or do, and don't let external influences affect your moods and state of mind. If you let people and external events affect your moods and state of mind, how can you focus your mind when you need to? It is true that it might not be easy to get rid of this habit, but if you learn to be aware of this subconscious habit, you will gradually be able to weaken its effect on you. Of course, don't forget that you also need to find some time every day to practice focus exercises.

Be Disciplined

Discipline is a method of training your mind, body or controlling your behavior. Discipline means obedience to a superior authority. Accepting the norms of the family, society, the commands of elders and obeying them is also discipline. Discipline means accepting punishments for violation. Discipline also means training of mind and character, developing self-control and the habit of obedience. In the entire universe, there is an order and discipline. The stars, the planets, the earth on which we live, the moon and the sun we see, move according to a system of discipline. We can see that plants, insects, birds and animals too observe discipline in their lives. Only man, who has a thinking mind, finds it difficult to observe discipline.

Discipline could be divided into two broad categories, external and internal. External discipline is that which is imposed by outside authority. It is often linked with authority and force. Discipline in the army is one such. Soldiers do not have a say in it except implicit obedience.

As Tennyson says "Theirs not to make reply. Theirs not to reason why. Theirs but to do and die". A soldier in a war field cannot ask for reasons. He has to obey commands; otherwise, the war is lost.

Our ancient educational system believed in enforcing discipline by force. They used to say, "If you spare the rod, you spoil the child". However, that view is not correct. It will produce only negative results. That is why discipline has taken a new shape in schools and colleges now. It is called self-discipline. It is discipline by acceptance, not by imposition.

Steps To Success

We live in a democracy. Democracy is based on the will of a majority of its citizens. It has to be accepted and obeyed. Otherwise democracy loses its meaning and leads to anarchy. Family customs and traditions, laws of the society, and moral and spiritual laws of the religion are all to be obeyed. That is discipline. Discipline demands obedience to commands from leaders, respect for women, devotion to God, etc. Though discipline starts at home, there is much more need for it in schools. Schools are nursing places for various virtues and values.

Discipline in the classroom, on the playground and elsewhere in the school is all important. Force has no place in student discipline. Teachers have to be disciplined, because one who cannot control oneself, cannot control others. Students emulate teachers in all ways. It is more so in the matter of discipline. They observe discipline by acceptance not by force. Some argue that discipline limits freedom and that kills the man's initiative. This is a wrong view. Lack of discipline cannot bring order. Self-discipline or discipline by acceptance is self-control. One controls one's emotions and desires and gives room to listen to other's points of view. Man has many desires and impulses. If they are allowed free play without discipline, it will end in chaos.

Nature and society are best disciplinarians. Violate their laws, and you are in for punishment. Put your finger in fire and it burns, no matter who you are. Thereby we learn discipline by experience. That is why Gandhi has rightly said that discipline is learnt in adversity. It is therefore necessary that if you wish to achieve anything enduring in life, you have to be first disciplined in life. Lack of discipline is like a ship without a rudder.

Value of Discipline

There is value of discipline in all walks of life. At school or at home, in the office or in the factory, in the playground or in the battlefield, discipline is a necessity. Discipline gives us an opportunity to learn, experience and grow. Without discipline, there will be complete chaos and disorder. There will be no peace and progress. To be guided by rules, to pay due regard to elders and superior officers, to obey them and to behave in an orderly manner, all these come under the term discipline.

In school, if the boys are not disciplined, the boys themselves will learn nothing and the very purpose of education will be defeated. Similarly, if the subordinates do not obey their senior officers in offices and factories, it will become difficult to carry on the work of production and administration. The office goers should maintain discipline and reach office in time. They are expected to complete their assignments within the allotted time. The country will not succeed if its public servants are not disciplined. There will be no plan and no organization. Similarly, if the army and the police refuse to carry out the orders of their generals and commanders, the enemy and the hooligans will have no difficulty in establishing their sway in the country. Thus, an undisciplined nation cannot expect to remain independent even for a moment.

Even in minor spheres, such as the home and the playground, people cannot do without discipline. If there were no discipline in the family, all the members of the family would go their own way. Then, there would be no peace and order in the family.

Steps To Success

Discipline is a good thing and there is no evil in it. It builds character, develops strength and unity and fosters co-operation. It is, therefore, necessary that children be taught discipline from their very childhood. It should never be overlooked, as it is the secret of success in life.

Discipline trains the mind in order to make it accept the rules and orders of a higher authority. It is a lesson that we can learn from the way the universe runs. Nature herself presents before us this valuable lesson. All the heavenly bodies follow definite rules in moving around. The seasons come and go in definite patterns. A slight shift or indiscipline will cause confusions in this well-planned natural system. Similarly, discipline in our individual lives is the top most requirement of our society.

The word discipline is derived from the Latin word 'discipulus' which means to learn. Discipline is the trait by which one learns to control one's feelings, emotions and behavior. It is the ability for self-control and self-direction. Discipline enables us to think maturely, act maturely and to take decisions responsibly. It makes us self-propelled, self- controlled and self-guiding persons. It makes us responsible persons and principled individuals.

Discipline is one of the essential qualities required for social living. Without it, life in society becomes chaotic and miserable. Without discipline, there can be no law and order. Without discipline society becomes a devil's paradise, where, 'might determines what is right' and power and riches determine who is right and who is not. Today, a quick look around us will show

how our society has come into the grips of chaos and confusions everywhere.

Lack of discipline in our lives is a primary cause of all these. Every profession, every service: politics, industry, economy, government, etc., need discipline. Discipline is often associated with men in uniform. It is the hallmark of soldiers. Discipline in the army calls for strict obedience and humble submission. It calls for duty in the face of adversity and courage in the face of odds. Without discipline no army can conquer, no army can win a war. That is why acts of indiscipline are most severely punished in the army.

This is one lesson which has to be learned at a very young age. The home is the first institution where the value of discipline can be learnt and the parents are the first guides. Then it is the responsibility of the teachers to inculcate in them the value of discipline. Today's students are tomorrow's leaders. Discipline will teach them the virtues of self-control, obedience, the capacity for self-sacrifice and single-minded devotion to duty. It is clear therefore, that discipline is not merely a good virtue, which adds color and charm to the personality. It is an essential quality of life required by every one of us. Discipline alone can lead our society forward and make our social, professional and family life, a successful one.

Meaning Of Self-Discipline

Self-discipline refers to the ability to control one's own feelings. It is a very important characteristic. Self-discipline leads one to overcome one's weaknesses. Life without self-discipline is no life. We need be guided by rules. We have to be respectful to our elders. We must obey our seniors. Its importance: Self-discipline is most needed for success in life. Discipline is necessary whether we are at school, home or at work. It is equally necessary whether we are in the office or on the playground. Our life, our society, our country or even the world will go astray without discipline. Therefore, some sort of discipline is required everywhere. There is order in Nature. Even small disorder in the world of Nature leads to chaos.

The formative days occur in schools and colleges. Self-discipline has to be learnt at every walk of life. Childhood is the best period for it. The young mind learns things quickly and easily. At school, the students are taught to behave well. They are taught to respect their elders. Even on the playground, the children are taught to follow the rules of the games. So the student days are the most formative period in which the value of self-discipline can be learnt.

Evils Of Indiscipline

A man is just like an animal without self-discipline. His life and actions become aimless. In the present age, lack of self-discipline is a great evil. It is growing in every walk of life. Both the young and the old do lawless acts. Today crimes and thefts are on the increase. People seem to have forgotten the value of self-discipline.

Causes Of Indiscipline

Lack of employment is a major cause of indiscipline and unrest. Over population makes the situation still worse. Overcrowding in schools and colleges causes indiscipline. Finally, poverty leads to disorder, unrest and indiscipline. In fact, self-discipline is a good thing. It builds character. It develops strength and unity. It creates a sense of co-operation. Therefore, self-discipline must be taught from the very childhood. It is a key to success in life. The higher is the sense of self-discipline, the better it is for the people and the country.

Be Committed

Commitment is the willingness to work hard and give your energy and time to do an activity or a job activity. Many people lead miserable lives. They are always pessimistic, exhausted and feeling very sad and angry. They live purposeless lives without any commitment just focusing on their pleasures and fun. They don't have any ambitions and never think about the future; their lives are meaningless. True life is not only pleasure and fun, but also it is a series of commitments first to God, then to ourselves, to our parents and our society. This is the concept which everyone should embrace.

First of all, a strong commitment to God and ourselves must be based on morals inspired from our religious beliefs and concepts. These religious concepts control our attitude towards other people as well as our relations with them. Moreover, we acquire ethics that build our personality by those beliefs. At the same time, we must have self-confidence and self-dependence to make the right choices and fulfill our dreams.

We must work hard to achieve our goals in all fields of life whether professional career, sports, arts or any other field. We must not let our lives pass by without reaching our purpose. Beside self-commitment and commitment to God, we must have a tight commitment to our parents. They spend their lives seeking our happiness and well- being. Thus we must be thankful and grateful to them. Our appreciation should be expressed by true love and care as well as good deeds. We must respect, obey them and help them whenever they need us. Moreover, when they grow old, we must be by their side to care for them and make sure they live in the best conditions possible by extending good health care, providing them financially whenever they need it and ensure their happiness.

Vince Lombardi said: "The quality of a person's life is directly proportional to their commitment to excellence, regardless of their chosen field of endeavor."

Superficiality in doing things is what produces results that cannot be trusted by other people. Such superficial activities have caused the biggest disasters of humanity and continue bringing harm to all the living beings. Performing excellence in the field a person chooses is the main key to a quality life which everybody tries to achieve. This quote is one of those that make people start thinking about what they do in their lives and the way they chose to do it. It has a lot to do with the conscience of a person.

No matter what a man chooses to do, he has two ways of doing it: properly or superficially. A person needs to do something on the proper level of excellence which it requires, or do nothing at all. There is no "golden middle" concerning this statement. All these lead to the quality of life that a person enjoys, not only in material or financial ways. The power of this quote is immense. It is more than just inspiration to the ones that not just read but also feel it. Following the advice that the quote carries may lead the person to experiencing the feeling of self-respect and respect of people around him. Even if a man works as a newspaper-deliverer and he presents his work at the best level, people will always say:" He is great at what he does". His boss will also say it and decide that this person is worthy of a better position. It is the law of life – only those who are the best at what they do achieve the biggest success. This quote is not just a law for all people, but it is a precaution for those who do not try their best at what they do. People should read it because it has the power to build a successful person in each of us.

Success and high quality of life go together not by luck, but because the inseparable part of the person's commitment to excellence affects both these factors regardless of the field that the person chooses. This quote is not even advice. It should become the main principle of life of every person. So, if a person decides to do something through hard work, dedication and commitment to excellence, the result will be not only a better quality of life but also a better quality of the personality of this person.

The reason I have selected this quote is because of the inspiration it gave me when I first read it. These words spoke to the depth of my heart and inspired me to be what I have always wanted to become. These words by Vince Lombardi make me remember that one day I will become old and I want to be proud of what I have done throughout my whole life and I will want to see the result of what I have done. I am glad that I can learn from people that have lived their lives and know what is really worthwhile at the end of it. I hope that I will always by mature enough to follow this testament of Vince Lombardi. This quote has helped me in the understanding that a man is a "real man" only if he is pure in his heart and insistent in his intentions.

I want to do everything in a way that I will never have to do it over again. Doing something over again will indicate that I did not show enough commitment to excellence. I try my best to apply it in every sphere of my life. If I am studying something I try not to do it superficially, but to do it in a manner that will make my teachers and me proud. The knowledge gained will open the doors for the work I have always dreamt about. I have understood that life is too short for doing anything not well enough.

Following the message of this quote will and is already making me a richer person, although not in the literal sense. This is primarily due to the fact that when I started doing everything with commitment to excellence I have learned many things. Now all of them seem easy to me though beforehand they seemed too difficult and almost impossible for me to do. I also realized how important it is to set this commitment to excellence to my academics.

This quote is capable for moving mountains because it has made an immense difference for me. I am not afraid of doing anything now because I know that my commitment to excellence will help me to do it.

Without my realizing it, commitment has become important in my daily life. Over time, it has determined the way I think about society. I hadn't really thought of it consciously, nor had I studied the concept or read about it before. Maybe now is the appropriate time to do so.

I don't use books or theories and what they have to say about commitment. I want to start from my own experience. I want to describe what commitment means to me in practice, but also in theory. Why an essay? Sometimes the written word, not only expresses a thought, but also the process of thinking itself. A process may be unfinished, but through writing about it we hold on to the thought. The written word can be resisted, can be negotiated and corrected without it fading or disappearing.

To begin with, one is expected to open with a definition. I do not believe in definitions. If we define concepts then we tend to think in solid terms, while concepts are always dynamic and can be differently defined. I do not want to sound post modernistic because I'm not, but I rather believe in outlining concepts than in defining them. Outlining the concepts that we use seems to me to be useful and especially meaningful.

Commitment means giving a piece of ourselves to what we do. It sounds simple but it is not. It's neither simple nor obvious. The obviousness got lost in the dominance of the 'everyone for his/her own' discourse. For those who cannot give that piece of himself or herself in his or her actions, it is difficult to understand why some of us do commit ourselves. Often we even cannot give an exact reason of why we are committed.
Commitment must be experienced and not explained. That is why my explanation here can never match the experience of commitment. So we can easily say what our commitment serves, but to explain the underlying reasons is far more difficult. No worries for whom this sounds familiar, for it is with time and in experiencing yourself in what you do, that one realizes what those reasons are.

Another aspect of commitment is the context. If we are only occupied with ourselves, it is all about our own context. By committing yourself, you realize that there is a broader context than your own. We realize that there are many things that are worthy of commitment. It becomes clear when you understand that commitment means 'Being in contact with the other' or

'Being busy with someone other than yourself. During our commitment, we must look beyond ourselves and step into a real relationship with the other. It is not a relationship where you find yourself lost or in which only the other exists. It is a constructive relationship where your commitment is and remains critical.

Commitment Begins Small And Can Get Bigger

In groups of two, three, four or more we come together with other people. These meetings give us the opportunity to look at our own reality from different perspectives, perspectives that without this commitment would be non-existent.

Equally important is the fact that through our commitment we obtain a place in the world. Through a commitment with and for others, we find a place for ourselves. A place for yourself in a broader context seems not only sensible, it's also badly needed in these times of fast living in which alienation has been internalized deep down. We can no longer stand on the sidelines as a spectator at an important part of our lives because like it or not, what happens in our environment has an impact on our lives. To live no longer as spectators but also as participants, means commitment is togetherness. You are together with others who also believe in commitment. This deep contact with others and the togetherness seems like a good exercise in cooperation, coexistence with the other. Through togetherness, searching for points of collaboration and connectedness is essential to make commitment succeed. One should not forget that one is committed to realize something, to change something. In addition, if inequality is the biggest problem in society, which is also ours, then change is essential. That does not mean I necessarily plead for a result-oriented commitment.

Steps To Success

Nowadays it seems fashionable that everything we do must be result-oriented.

Commitment is first and foremost a process in which one can engage with other people, in which one can listen and learn from others and thus widens their horizon. Therefore, one must experience commitment, because only in the experience one can see the value and importance of being committed. Value and importance benefit not only the person to whom one is committed, but also oneself. Commitment is apart from giving or taking.

I believe that each of us gains much if committed to the place where one lives and to the people with whom one lives. When you build a relationship with other people and find something in common, it feels good. You feel at home, at ease. That does not mean that commitment should remain purely local or where you live at the moment. I think it is important that we commit ourselves where our daily life takes place in the districts, villages and cities where we live together. It is there we can do something, because we can change something. However, this does not have to be in conflict with a commitment in a wider area. We should be committed, connected and in solidarity with people around the world who engage themselves for change and improvement as well to all the goals that we want to achieve. Your beginning might be small, but I assure you that if you can be committed to your goals, your dreams, and hopes for the future, you will get there in the end.

Avoid your Enemy Of Success: Laziness

What is laziness? It is the desire to be idle, to do nothing and resist effort. It is a state of passivity and of letting things stay as they are. Sometimes, we enjoy being a little lazy, such as after working hard for several hours, or on a very cold or warm day, but if this state occurs too often, something has to be done about it. In order to carry out our chores, work efficiently, live to the fullest, and achieve success, we must learn how to overcome laziness.

Simple Steps For Overcoming Laziness

Break Down A Task Into Smaller Tasks

We often avoid tasks because we find them too big, too overwhelming, too tiring, or taking too much of our time. Breaking a task into several smaller tasks can solve this problem. Then, each one will not seem so difficult or intimidating. Instead of having one big task, we will have a series of small tasks which do not require too much effort. This approach can be applied not only to tasks, but also to goals and everything else we have or need to do. This will tend to melt much of the laziness and inner resistance we often experience.

Rest, Sleep And Exercise

In some cases, laziness is due to being tired and lacking energy. If this is true in your case, you need to give yourself the rest and sleep you need, and also give your body enough exercise and fresh air.

Strengthen Your Willpower & Self-discipline

Learn how to strengthen your willpower (determination) and self-discipline, overcome procrastination, laziness and indecisiveness, and increase your inner strength with perseverance and patience.

Motivation

In some cases, the reason for laziness is due to lack of motivation. You can strengthen your motivation through affirmations, visualization and thinking about the importance of performing your task or chore or achieving your goal and thinking about what will happen to you if the goal or task is not achieved.

Have A Vision Of What And Who You Want To Be

Frequently reflecting on the person we want to be, the goals we want to achieve, and the life we want to live, can motivate us to act. This will remind you that if you don't act to fulfill your vision and to march towards who you want to be, you may end up not being who you want to be.

Think About Benefits

Think about the benefits you will gain if you overcome your laziness and take action, instead of thinking about the difficulties or obstacles. Focusing on the difficulties of carrying out the task, leads to discouragement, avoidance of taking action and to laziness. It is important that you focus your mind and attention on the benefits, not on the difficulties.

Thinking About The Consequences

Think about what will happen, if you succumb to laziness, and don't perform your task or chore. Thinking about the consequences of not acting, can also push you to take action.

Steps To Success

Doing One Thing At A Time
Focus on doing one thing at a time. If you feel you have a lot to do, you will probably feel overwhelmed and let laziness overcome you, instead of you overcoming laziness.

Visualization
Your imagination has a great influence on your mind, habits and action. Visualize yourself performing the task easily, energetically and enthusiastically. Do so before starting with a task or goal, and also when you feel lazy, or when your mind whispers to you to abandon what you are doing. Ignore negative thoughts that may come into your mind by then.

Repeat Affirmations
Tell yourself: "I can accomplish my goal." "I have the energy and motivation to act and do whatever I want or have to do." "Doing things makes me stronger." "Doing things makes things happen."

Regard A Task As An Exercise
Consider each task as an exercise to make you stronger, more decisive and more assertive and this will increase your success creativity skills.

Procrastination
Avoid procrastination, the murderer of time and a form of laziness. If there is something you have to do, why not do it right now and get through with it? Why let it stay nagging at the back of your head? The best time to do anything is now and at its appointed time. Laziness, as well, makes us to do things that we didn't intend to do with our time.

For example, if you are a student and you are too lazy to study and don't feel like it. How is it that you can be able to spend your time from that point of laziness by socializing on Whatsapp, Facebook, Twitter or updating your Facebook time line? Or spend your time watching TV, sleeping or doing other things that are not part of the plan? By doing so, you'll be using the time that you could use to be successful in life. If you are extravagant with your time, you are unlikely to make it to success.

Learn From Successful People
Watch successful people and see how they do not let laziness win. Learn from them, talk with them and associate with them.

Overcoming the habit of laziness is achieved through a series of daily actions and activities, when you choose to act, instead of remaining passive. Every time you overcome your laziness you get stronger. Every time you choose to act, you increase your ability to win, achieve goals and improve your life.

Steps To Time Management Success

Everyone one of us is given 24 hours a day, 365 days a year. Time is money. Time is precious. Time wasted is lost forever. One thing that you have to be strict with yourself in your life in order to be successful is time. Time is very crucial. Time waits for no man and time can never be recovered. If you fail to plan and manage your time, you have failed to plan and manage your life.

Is your day overloaded with meetings, managing your business, planning for the future and day-to-day work? Do you get to the end of the day and wonder what you really accomplished? Is your work day overflowing into your home life? Do you wish you could get a handle on time management once and for all, so you could run your life rather than your life running you? You're not alone. Don't let the march of time spin you into a tizzy of stress and desperation. Apply these top seven Steps and watch your time expand to include what's most important to you.

Prioritize—Put Your "Rocks" In First

What's most important to you? Building your business? Getting a promotion? Leaving work at 5 p.m.? Studying a book? You need to focus on your priorities, the things that matter the most to you. Identify your top priorities right now. These are the "rocks" that you put in your schedule before adding lower-priority items.

Target Your Action

Do your action items line up with your priorities, the rocks that you just defined? If they don't, you're spending your time on non-priorities. Once you determine what the rocks are, scan your vast to-do list. For example: (1) Work on new project, (2) Contact 10 past clients, (3) Have meeting with boss about promotion, for those working.

To those who are students: You'll have to create your own study time table and stick to time table. As well, add some time to rest and do your chores.

Go to work on these priority tasks. When you complete them, address others on the to-do list. Don't get side-tracked by unimportant things. Learn to prioritize and stick to your list. Be honest and productive about what you really need to be done now.

Focus Your Mind First

Consider focusing your mind as a warm-up before stepping onto the field. When you wake up, do you hit the snooze bar 7 times? When you do finally get up, do you jump out of bed, gulp a cup of coffee and run out the door? How you start the morning is a reflection of how you live your life. Instead, start your day with 15 minutes in which you focus your mind in solitude. Your brain will sharpen and your productivity will increase just from this one step.

Take Something Off Your Plate

Okay, you've calmed your mind in the morning. You feel sharp and ready to go. Now look at your week, your month, your entire work or school schedule and remove something. Review the things you do regularly that consume too much of your time or drain you. Do you have to do them personally? Can you outsource them? Are these things important, or are you just in the habit of doing them without thinking? Remember the priorities that you set. The truth is, there are many things on your lists that are not urgent and not important. Remember: just because you're good at it doesn't mean you have to do it!

Complete Something You've Been Putting Off

Shorten your to-do list. If you let things pile up, they'll rob you of time when you need it most. Get something done that's been on your list day after day. This will immediately refuel your energy and free up mental space to focus on priorities. Clear off your desk or return a phone call. Then pause and take a moment to enjoy the satisfaction of getting things done. Take one hour this week to complete something you've been putting off.

Declare Yourself Complete

"Finish each day and be done with it." Ralph Waldo Tex Johnstone says this step is key. If you face the end of the day and 185 unanswered e- mails still sit in your inbox, say to yourself, "I declare myself complete." This sends a signal to your brain that you're done. Free yourself to let go and move on with the rest of your day. Your days could, and sometimes do, extend into twelve, fourteen or even more hours. Save time for the rest of your life too. You'll be happier and more productive.

Accept That You Can't Do It All At Once

"What? But I want to do it all!" you may say. This one can be hard to agree to, especially if you're passionate about work and life. Remember that what you take on can take place over a period of time. It doesn't all have to occur right now. Once you realize and accept that you can't do it all right now, you'll experience immediate relief and free up new hours in your week.

Do what matters most with quality, then move on to the next thing. Now that you've discovered these 7 steps to time management, schedule time for one, two or three of them into your calendar today. Start practicing these skills right away. You'll spend less stress and energy on things that don't matter, and gain more time for the important things in life. Remember, "If you fail to plan and manage your time, you've failed to plan and manage your life".

Ten Steps To Your Success

The desire to achieve success is inherent in every human being. It is the desire to grow, do more, achieve more, and to make one's dreams come true. Your dreams can become your reality, if you have a strong desire and are determined to succeed. Here are a few motivational tips which I hope will help you on your journey to success.

Imagination Often Turns Into Reality

Imagine a certain situation over and again, with love and joy, and sooner or later you will attract it into your life, provided you don't let contradictory thoughts enter your mind. Start with simple situations first, to gain faith and experience with this process.

What You Do Every Day Will Turn Into A Habit

Choose habits that will lead you to success and repeat them every day. In time, they will become automatic, not requiring thought, attention or effort. There are many new habits you can adopt, such as positive thinking, being on time, being more considerate, and getting a stronger willpower or staying calm in difficult situations.

Don't Let Moods Control your Life

Letting moods control your life is like sitting in a boat and letting the waves and currents take you wherever they please. Developing inner strength and self-discipline is like attaching a powerful engine to your boat. With this powerful engine, you will be able to navigate the boat of your mind wherever you want.

Steps To Success

Break The Obstacles In Your Way

Sometimes the right thing to do is to break the obstacles in your way. At other times, a better course of action would be to climb over the obstacle. There are times, when to go around it is to be recommended. Sometimes, it would be wiser to find a completely new route, new direction.

Never Lose Hope

No matter how bleak things look, hope is the rope that will pull you up. It is your connection, your stairway, to get your dreams and expectations realized. Never leave the rope of hope.

Read Between The Lines

When reading inspirational books, articles or quotes, strive to read between the lines. This is where intuition and wisdom will arise and bring greater truths. The words lead you to the understanding. Reading between the words leads you to wisdom.

Take Positive Action

To get positive results from positive thinking, you should also take positive action. Positive thinking will make you happy, good-natured and optimistic. It will also make you aware of opportunities. Positive action would make positive thinking work for you and bring the results you want. Take action to make things happen. This is positive thinking in action.

It Doesn't Matter Where You Live

Even if you live in poor or faraway place, you can achieve success. With a focused and clear goal, strong desire, and the use of visualization and affirmations, you will get where you want. With belief and determination, you can make the necessary changes in your life. Affirmations, words with power guidance, instructions, and many affirmations for every purpose, help you find love, attract money, succeed in business, get rid of negative habits, increase self-confidence, and much more.

Treat Your Time Like Money In The Bank

What do you spend your time on? Don't waste your time. Use it correctly. Every day that passes is like an amount of money that you withdrew from your account. If you are careful with your money, you should be also careful with your time. Spend it on something that helps you, adds value to your life, gets you somewhere, and helps other people.

Adopt An Attitude Of Calmness And Of Open-Mindedness

Such an attitude would make it easier for you to see new opportunities, conceive new ideas, focus on goals, and see things from a different point of view. This will increase your chances of achieving success.

No Sacrifices No Success

Success requires hard work, investing energy, time and sweat and all that it takes. Success doesn't go where it is not needed; neither does it stay where it not appreciated. Success involves starting something small and nurturing it like a flower, doing all you can to make sure you help it where it matters.

Failure is an orphan, but success comes with many family members. Success will attract many things and many people, but only those who are worthy and can contribute to make the success last are worthy of being allowed to stay.

Success also comes with many enemies. To stay successful, managing enemies is an important skill.

Success does not come cheap as many believe. It comes at a cost. Sacrifices must be made and the sacrifices cost in time, energy and hard work.

Only hard work leads to success. Don't sleep around and expect success to run after you.

The Ten Commandments Of Success

Success belongs to everybody and anybody who is willing and ready to give it a good shot and go after it. It is not reserved to a few selected individuals. There are certain principles or commandments that need to be followed in order to record and be a success.

It does not matter how you start. How you start does not determine how successful you will become. There is a psychological tendency in humans always to improve as the day goes by. Always remember that slow and steady wins the race. Nobody cares how you start, what people care about is the end result.

Having a winning mentality and the right attitude is crucial to being successful. You must have the winning mentality. Nobody can become successful without believing in his or her ability to deliver. Never doubt your capability. Try to give your best to be a winner always.

Here are the commandments of success.

Welcome Criticism

Whenever you set out to do something original, daring, important and exciting there will always be people who will try to talk you out of it. They will tell you your idea or goal is crazy, unrealistic, too risky, too innovative, and too strange. Take it as possible feedback, not as the absolute truth, because in most cases people's criticism has nothing to do with your goal and everything to do with their own personal fears, doubts and negative past experiences.

Steps To Success

Learn From Your Failures

The more attempts you take at something, the sooner you will figure out the best way of doing it. Do not be afraid to try and fail. In fact, welcome failure; learn from it and try again. Failure gives you experience to do things in a better way, as well with determination. It gives you the willpower to try it with more effort.

Dream Big

Every important achievement always starts with a great dream. Do not settle for less, just because it is easy, familiar and guaranteed. At some point in your life you will have to face a decision to take a risk and go for an opportunity or settle for less than you know you are capable of achieving.

"Aim for the sky and you will reach the ceiling. Aim for the ceiling you will stay on the floor". Bill Shankly says, "Love what you do in order to be successful." It is important to love what you do. Success does not solely imply financial security and a handsome paycheck at the end of the month. It is about self-realization and enjoyment as well.

Always Open Your Mind To Possibilities

It is not always easy to spot a great opportunity that comes your way, especially when it looks like a problem, but this does not mean that we should stop trying. Be careful not to become too rigid in your thinking, as it will impede your ability to see possibilities and act on them.

Always Be Time Conscious

If you want to be successful in life, you have to see every new day, every minute of your life as an opportunity for growth and achievement. Make it a habit of asking yourself throughout the day "Am I doing something meaningful or useful?" If not, you are stealing from yourself one of the most precious treasures you have been given – your time.

Associate With Winners

The people in your life will to some extent determine how successful you will be. Always associate and exchange ideas with winners and people who share the same dream as you.

Encourage Others

Starting today, focus on empowering instead of judging, helping instead of criticizing, listening instead of talking, learning instead of convincing that your opinion is the only correct one in the room, and something magical will happen. People will follow you, seek your advice and offer their help to you without you having to ask for it.

Avoid Distractions

A great way of dealing with distractions is to remind yourself that they are the main reason why you will feel stressed out, overwhelmed and unproductive by the end of the week. Every time you say "No" to distractions, you are moving one-step closer to becoming a true master of your time and success. For that purpose, avoid distraction at all cost.

Develop The Action Habit

Don't be a man of words but a man of action. To be successful in life you have to start taking action and not only talking about what you intend to do. Take the risk; do what you need to do.

Be Patient

Success does not come overnight and it does not just happen. It takes time. It needs planning. Being patient is very important in

Steps To Success

becoming successful. Success is a process and you must love all the process involved. Give back to society and visualize your success. Sharing is caring.

Follow Your Passions and Success Will Follow

Whether you're thinking about starting something that will earn you a living such as a business or thinking about what career path to choose, it's important that you follow your passions. When we think about what is needed to be successful in life and in our work, we usually think about characteristics such as value, talent, ambition, intellect, discipline, persistence and luck. What many of us often fail to include in this recipe for success is passion. The passion we have or do not have for our work should not be underestimated. Sometimes this ingredient makes the biggest difference of all.

Before I describe what I mean by passion and why it's so important, we must first explore what the true meaning of success is a bit further. Success is usually assumed to be associated with large sums of wealth or a high level of fame, but true success is not all about money, Success is, or at least should be, primarily defined as an achievement of something desired. Therefore, the most successful people are the ones who achieve the things they most desire. What we desire the most, even more than money, is to be proud of what we do with our lives. This is especially true when it comes to our work.

A truly successful person is one who is proud of the work he or she does. That is the true meaning of success. Making a lot of money shouldn't be the primary definition of success, but it is a reasonable goal to have. We all want to have enough money to sustain our family and ourselves. Actually, if we are truly passionate about the work we do, there's probably a better chance that money will follow.

Steps To Success

What I Mean By Passion

When I speak of passion, I don't mean it in the romantic way. What I mean by passion is the powerful feeling of enthusiasm we all have inside of us. We are all enthusiastic and passionate about something, whether it is finance, food or a favorite sport. That enthusiasm is very powerful. When we can combine it with our work, we are setting ourselves up well for achieving true success.

Why Passion Is So Important

When we are enthusiastic and proud of the work we do, we are better equipped to overcome the many obstacles that will surely arise in the process of starting a business or moving up in a career. Also, the more enthusiasm we have, the more inclined we are to work harder at improving ourselves. This will allow us to continuously get better at the work we do. The better we get at our work, the better we can get paid for doing it. Ensuring we are passionate about our work will not only provide us with a meaningful career, but it will also give us a good chance of being paid well. The passion we have for our work can be the difference between making a living or making a killing.

The Successful Of Our Time

Steve Jobs

One of the most successful companies in the world today is Apple. When we think of Apple we also think of Apple's ex-CEO, the late Steve Jobs. Carmine Gallo wrote an article called "The Seven Success Principles of Steve Jobs," which outlines seven key factors that are responsible for Jobs' success. The article is based on multiple interviews with Apple employees and Steve Jobs himself.

Believe it or not, the No. 1 principle in this article is, "do what you love." Steve Jobs believed in the power of passion, and once said, "People with passion can change the world for the better." Jobs claimed that the passion he had for his work made all the difference.

Chris Gardner

Chris Gardner, the once homeless man turned multi-millionaire stockbroker that Will Smith plays in the movie, "The Pursuit of Happiness", once expressed what he believes is the secret to success. He stated that he believes the secret is to "find something you love to do so much, you can't wait for the sun to rise to do it all over again." He explains that the most inspiring leaders are those who don't work at a job, but pursue a calling. This is like what I explained in my first book titled, "Destiny is matter of Choice". If you want to be rich, think of becoming an employer, not an employee.

Mark Zuckerberg

These days we cannot talk about success without mentioning Facebook and Facebook's CEO, Mark Zuckerberg. The 27-year old billionaire has changed the world we live in. In David

Steps To Success

Kirkpatrick's book, "The Facebook Effect: The Inside Story of The Company That is Connecting The World," Kirkpatrick lists what he believes are Zuckerberg ingredients for success.

One of these ingredients is, you guessed it, follow your passion - not money. Zuckerberg suggests to "following your happiness," and explains that even if you don't end up making a fortune, you'll at least be doing what you love.

Warren Buffett

Warren Buffett, known as "the Oracle of Omaha" and probably one of the greatest investors of all time, usually talks about his secrets to successful investing, but even Buffett knows there is more to success than money. One of his articles, "10 Ways To Get Rich: Warren Buffett's Secret That Can Work For You," Buffet ends off his list of advice with, "know what success really means." He explains the importance of finding what it is that brings true meaning to our lives, what makes each day important and to make this our focus.

As well you may be surprised as a young man how I got all this information about these successful people. It is my passion for success that led me into having zeal to know the secret to their kind of success.

It's Never Too Late

For those of us who have been thinking, "I'm already following my passion" while reading this book, that's great! You should appreciate that because you're in the minority. According to my research, over 50% employees were dissatisfied with their jobs in 2009 here in South Africa. It stated that most South Africans were only working for their current employer simply because they had to.

Now, obviously most of us have to work one way or another (unless you were born into riches and are completely spoiled). So, don't just quit your day job because you aren't completely satisfied. However, that doesn't mean you can't pursue another more fulfilling career path part time. Have you ever heard the saying, "it's never too late to be what you could've been?" Well, it's true. If you have an idea of where you want to be, you can still make moves towards getting there. If you have a full-time job to support you while you make that transition, which may actually be even better.

True success is much more than having a lot of wealth and fame. Enjoying the work you do is, in some ways, more important than having a large bank account. Plus, if you enjoy the work you do, there's a greater chance you will do great work and get paid accordingly. If you're thinking about starting your own business, or just struggling with this in your own personal career, you may need to think about what you're passionate about. It may not be easy, but chances are it will be worth the effort.

Why Success Always Starts With Failure

Although success may start with failure, we certainly don't act as though it does. When our mistakes stare us in the face, we often find it so upsetting that we miss out on the primary benefit of failing (yes, benefit): the chance to get over our egos and come back with a stronger, smarter approach. Success comes through rapidly fixing our mistakes rather than getting things right first time.

The Wrong Way To React To Failure

When it comes to failing, our egos are our own worst enemy. As soon as things start going wrong, our defense mechanisms kick in, tempting us to do what we can to save face. Yet, these very normal reactions of denial, chasing your losses, and hedonic editing wreak havoc on our ability to adapt.

Denial

It seems to be the hardest thing in the world to admit we've made a mistake and try to put it right. It requires you to challenge a status quo of your own making.

Chasing your losses

We're so anxious not to "draw a line under a decision we regret" that we end up causing still more damage while trying to erase it. For example, poker players who've just lost some money are primed to make riskier bets than they'd normally take in a hasty attempt to win the lost money back and "erase" the mistake.

Hedonism

When we engage in hedonism, we try to convince ourselves that the mistake doesn't matter, bundling our losses with our gains or finding some way to reinterpret our failures as successes. We are so anxious not to "draw a line under a decision we regret" that we end up causing still more damage while trying to erase it.

The Recipes For Success

Adaptation

We must use an adaptive, experimental approach to succeed We can't begin to predict whether our "great idea" will actually sink or swim once it's out there. You have to cast a wide net, "practice failing" in a safe space, and be primed to let go of your idea if you've missed the mark.

Try new things

"Expose yourself to lots of different ideas and try lots of different approaches, on the grounds that failure is common." Experiment where failure is survivable.

"Look for experimental approaches where there is much to learn, such as, for example, projects with small downsides but bigger upsides. Too often we take on projects where the cost of failure is prohibitive and just hope for the best. Recognize when you haven't succeeded.

"The third principle is the easiest to state and the hardest to stick to: know when you've failed." The more complex and elusive our problems are, the more effective trial and error becomes.

Recognize Failure

This is the hard part. We've been trained that persistence pays off, so it feels wrong to cut our losses and label an idea a failure. However, if you're truly self-aware and listening closely after a "release" of your idea, you can't go wrong. Being able to recognize a failure just means that you'll be able to re-cast it into something more likely to succeed.

Gather feedback
"Above all, feedback is essential for determining which experiments have succeeded and which have failed. Get advice, not just from one person, but from several."

If the feedback is harsh, be objective. "Take the venom out," and dig out the real advice.

Remove emotions from the equation
"It's important to be dispassionate: forget whether you're ahead or behind, and try to look at the likely costs and benefits of continuing from when you are."

Don't get too attached to your plan
There's nothing wrong with having a plan, but remember that no plan survives first contact with the enemy. The danger is a plan that seduces us into thinking failure is impossible and adaptation is unnecessary. Being able to recognize a failure just means that you'll be able to re-cast it into something more likely to succeed.

Steps To Success

Achieving True Success And Prosperity

True Success

Success is not a simple matter; it cannot be determined merely by the amount of money and material possessions you have. The meaning of success goes far deeper. It can only be measured by the extent to which your inner peace and mental control enable you to be happy under all circumstances. That is real success. The secret of success and happiness is inside you. If you have found success and prosperity outside, but not inside, you are not truly successful. A millionaire who is not happy is not successful. I don't mean that if you have a million dollars you cannot be a success. Whether you are rich or poor, if you get happiness out of life you are a real success. Nothing is impossible, unless you think it is.

As a mortal being, you are limited, but as a child of God, you are unlimited. Focus your attention on God and you shall have all the power you want to use in any direction. Will is the instrument of the image of God within you. In his will lies His limitless power, the power that controls all the forces of nature. As you are made in His image, that power is yours to bring about whatever you desire. When you make up your mind to do good things, you will accomplish them if you use dynamic will power to follow through. No matter what the circumstances are, if you go on trying, God will create the means by which your will shall find its proper reward. Jesus referred this truth to when he said:

"If ye have faith, and doubt not, if ye shall say unto this mountain, be thou removed, and be thou cast into the sea, it shall be done."

Steps To Success

If you continuously use your willpower no matter what reverses come, it will produce success and health and power to help people, and above all, it will produce communion with God. Mortal man's brain is full of "cant's." Being born in a family with certain characteristics and habits, he is influenced by these to think he can't do certain things; he can't walk much, he can't eat this, he can't stand that. Those "cant's" have to be cauterized. You have within you the power to accomplish everything you want; that power lies in the will. If you cling to a certain thought with dynamic willpower, it finally assumes a tangible outward form.

Carrying a thought with dynamic will power, means holding to it until the thought pattern develops dynamic force. When a thought is made dynamic by will force, it can manifest according to the mental image you have created.

How Can You Develop Will For Success?

Choose some objective that you think you cannot accomplish, and then try with all your might to do that one thing. When you have achieved success, go on to something bigger and keep on exercising your will power in this way. If your difficulty is great, deeply pray: "Lord, give me the power to conquer all my difficulties." You must use your will power, no matter what you are, or who you are. You must make up your mind. Use this will power both in business and in meditation. Success or failure is determined in your own mind. Even against the negative opinion of the rest of society, if you bring out by your all-conquering God-given will the conviction that you cannot be left to suffer in difficulties, you will feel a secret divine power coming upon you; and you will see that the magnetism of that conviction and power is opening up new ways for you.

Dealing Constructively With Failure

The season of failure is the best time for sowing the seeds of success. The bludgeon of circumstances may bruise you, but keep your head erect. Always try once more, no matter how many times you have failed. Fight when you think that you can fight no longer, or when you think that, you have already done your best, or until your efforts are crowned with success. Learn how to use the psychology of victory. Some people advise, "Don't talk about failure at all." But that alone won't help. First, analyze your failure and its causes, benefit from the experience, and then dismiss all thought of it. Though he might fail many times, the man who keeps on striving, who is undefeated within, is a truly victorious person.

Life may be dark, difficulties may come, opportunities may slip by unutilized, but never within yourself say, "I am done for. God has forsaken me." Who could do anything for that kind of person? Your family may forsake you; good fortune may seemingly desert you; all the forces of man and nature may be arrayed against you; but by the quality of divine initiative within you, you can defeat every invasion of fate created by your own past wrong actions, and march victorious into paradise. No matter how many times you fail, keep on trying. No matter what happens, if you have unalterably resolved, "The earth may be shattered, but I will keep on doing the best I can," you are using dynamic will, and you will succeed. That dynamic will is what makes one man rich and another man strong and another man a saint.

Steps To Success

Don't Do Half-Heartedly

Most people do everything half-heartedly. They use only about one-tenth of their attention. That is why they don't have the power to succeed. Do everything with the power of attention. The full force of that power can be attained through meditation. When you use that focusing power of God, you can place it on anything and be a success.

Be Creative

Tune yourself with the creative power of Spirit. You will be in contact with the Infinite Intelligence that is able to guide you and to solve all problems. Power from the dynamic source of your being will flow uninterruptedly so that you will be able to perform creatively in any sphere of activity. Ask yourself this question: "Have I ever tried to do anything that nobody else has done?" That is the starting point in the application of initiative.

If you haven't thought that far, you are like hundreds of others who erroneously think they have no power to act differently than they do. They are like sleepwalkers; the suggestions coming from their subconscious mind have given them the consciousness of one-horsepower people.

If you have been going through life in this somnambulistic state, you must wake yourself by affirming: "I have man's greatest quality: initiative. Every human being has some spark of power by which he can create something that has not been created before.

Yet I see how easily I could be deluded with the mortal consciousness of limitation that pervades the world, if I allowed myself to be hypnotized by environment! What is initiative? It is

63

a creative faculty within you, a spark of the Infinite Creator. It may give you the power to create something no one else has ever created. It urges you to do things in new ways. The accomplishments of a person of initiative may be as spectacular as a shooting star. Apparently creating something from nothing, he demonstrates that the seemingly impossible may become possible by one's employment of the great inventive power of the Spirit. The one who creates does not wait for an opportunity, blaming circumstances, the fates, and the gods. He seizes opportunities or creates them with the magic wand of his will, effort, and searching discrimination.

Before embarking on important undertakings, sit quietly, calm your senses and thoughts, and meditate deeply. You will then be guided by the great creative power of Spirit. Whenever you want to produce something, do not depend upon the outside source; go deep and seek the Infinite Source. All methods of business success, all inventions, all vibrations of music, and all inspirational thoughts and writings are recorded in the annals of God.

Creating All-Round Success

He who seeks God is the wisest. He is the most successful who has found God. Great teachers will never counsel you to be neglectful; they will teach you to be balanced. You have to work, no doubt, to feed and clothe the body, but if you allow one duty to contradict another, it is not true duty. Thousands of businessmen are so busy gathering wealth, they forget that they are creating a lot of heart disease too! If duty to prosperity makes you forget duty to health, it is not duty. One should develop in a harmonious way. There is no use giving special attention to developing a wonderful body, if it houses a peanut brain. The mind also must be developed. And if you have excellent health and prosperity and intellect, but you are not happy, then you have still not made a success of your life. When you can truthfully say, "I am happy, and no one can take my happiness away from me," you are a king and you have found the image of God within you.

Another qualification of success is that we not only bring harmonious and beneficial results to ourselves, but also share those benefits with others. Life should be chiefly service. Without that ideal, the intelligence that God has given you is not reaching out toward its goal. When in service you forget the little self, you will feel the big Self of Spirit. As the vital rays of the sun nurture all, so should you spread rays of hope in the hearts of the poor and forsaken, kindle courage in the hearts of the despondent, and light a new strength in the hearts of those who think that they are failures. When you realize that life is a joyous battle of duty and at the same time a passing dream, and when you become filled with the joy of making others happy by giving them kindness and peace, in God's eyes your life is a success.

Abundance And Prosperity
Those who seek prosperity for themselves alone are in the end bound to become poor or to suffer from mental disorder, but those who consider the whole world as their home, and who really care and work for group or world prosperity find the individual prosperity that is legitimately theirs. This is a sure and secret law. Every day, do some good to help others, even if it is only a pittance. If you want to love God, you must love people. They are His children. You can be helpful materially by giving to the needy; and mentally by giving comfort to the

sorrowful, courage to the fearful, divine friendship and moral support to the weak.

You also sow seeds of goodness when you interest others in God, and cultivate in them greater love for God, deeper faith in Him. When you leave this world, material riches will be left behind; but every good that you have done will go with you. Wealthy people who live in miserliness, and selfish people who never help others, do not attract wealth in their next life. But those who give and share, whether they have much or little, will attract prosperity. That is the law of God. Think of Divine Abundance as a mighty, refreshing rain; whatever receptacle you have at hand will receive it. If you hold up a tin cup, you will receive only that quantity. If you hold up a bowl, that will be filled.

What kind of receptacle are you holding up to Divine Abundance? Perhaps your vessel is defective; if so, it should be repaired by casting out all fear, hate, doubt, and envy, and then cleansed by the purifying waters of peace, tranquility, devotion, and love. Divine Abundance follows the law of service and generosity. Give and then receive. Give to the world the best you have and the best will come back to you.

Affirmations For Success

Affirmation theory and instructions I will go forth in perfect faith in the power of Omnipresent God to bring me what I need at the time I need it. Within me is the Infinite Creative Power. I shall not go to the grave without some accomplishments. I am a God-man, a rational creature. I am the power of Spirit, the dynamic Source of my soul. I shall create revelations in the world of business, in the world of thought, in the world of wisdom. I and my Father are One. I can create anything I desire, even as my creative Father.

Other Books by this Author

1. Destiny is a Matter of Choice
2. The Power Of Determination

To order any of the books

Email: Blessed.btm@gmail.com
Cell: O61 953 9726/ 078506 5555

Download the kindle version or order a printed paperback copy on Amazon.com

(Type the name of the book or Author on the search bar).

The Publisher

Email: williamhenryjenkins@gmail.com

www.ingramcontent.com/pod-product-compliance
Lightning Source LLC
Chambersburg PA
CBHW071627040426
42452CB00009B/1518